# INSPIRATIONAL TERRACING

**Terrace Design in Structural Landscaping**

## By Paul Nordmark

Kirk House Publishers
Minneapolis, Minnesota

## Inspirational Terracing

Terrace Design in Structural Landscaping
By Paul Nordmark

Photography courtesy of Paul Nordmark.

Library of Congress Cataloging-in-Publication Data

Nordmark, Paul, 1965-
  Inspirational terracing : terrace design in structural landscaping / by Paul Nordmark
      p. cm.
  ISBN 1-886513-40-6 (alk. paper)
1.  Stone in landscape gardening 2. Landscape design. 3. Terracing. I. Title.
  SB475.5 .N67 2001
  717--dc21
2001050487

Kirk House Publishers, PO Box 390759, Minneapolis, MN 55439
www.kirkhouse.com
Manufactured in the United States of America

# CONTENTS

NOTE: *Specific information regarding materials used in the landscape projects shown in this book is printed on page 72.*

# DEDICATION

This book is dedicated to all the people for whom I have built terraces, and who have given me permission to include photographs of those terraces. It is also dedicated to those for whom these structural landscape ideas will become an inspiration.

The book is also dedicated to my family who lives with my passion to create living pictures for people to enjoy.

And it is dedicated to the One to whom I gave my life as a teenager, Jesus Christ. He has influenced my life that my work may become a blessing for many.

# FOREWORD

This is a book on landscape terracing. It is not a book on retaining walls. There are many different styles of landscaping and many different materials that can be used to build terraces.

My education did not include formal instruction in terrace landscaping. However, in the course of my landscape work I have developed a terracing technique which I call structural landscaping. Structural landscaping is the combination of a series of structures which become a terrace through the use of a terracing material chosen to bring a certain color or order to the surroundings of a home, building, or property. The structural design has a purpose and practical usefulness related to the plantings and flowers which will complete the landscape project. A well maintained terrace is a thing of beauty, to be enjoyed.

The terms used in this book to identify the terracing structures are names I have coined in my experience as a landscaping terrace builder. To my knowledge, no one else uses these landscaping terms. Identifying the distinctive ways of doing different techniques is helpful to me as I plan terracing. The terms are helpful in working with clients to get an idea of what styles or techniques they like or dislike. These terms have given me a whole new way to present my work.

The terracing terms are helpful in identifying the landscape structures that are suggested by the terrain in front of a home. Of course, there are several structural designs that could be used and a number of material combinations which become the options for the terrace design. But, what does the homeowner like? The difficulty of explaining to homeowners the options of the different styles and techniques of terracing is diminished with the use of the terms. Pages five through eleven are a visual glossary of the structural landscaping terms. You will see how I identify structures in terracing. When you begin your terracing project these structures will come alive to you. As you study the terrain and see the different options it provides, you will want to return to these pages to use the techniques that apply to your terracing situation.

I have designed and built every terrace pictured in this book. There are endless terracing possibilities when you use your own God-given creative talents to come up with the designs. A beautiful terrace begins with looking at the bare piece of ground and "seeing" what characteristics of that space are appropriate to the various structural designs. To begin, study with an open mind the terrain where you would like to build a terrace. You may be surprised by a design you wouldn't have imagined.

The terrace will come together one stone at a time, and ideas will come as you work. Many options may present themselves as you begin working your way into the slope of the terrain. In the end you will have created a beautiful terrace that can be planted to complete the landscape project.

# Terracing

Terracing is a method of creating level planting areas on a sloping hillside or on flat ground, with the addition of good soil.

Every terrace design is approached differently depending on what you are trying to accomplish and on the location of the project. Where you begin your terrace walls depends on whether your terrace is at the foundation of your house around existing stairs, or isolated some distance from your home.

To create a terrace you will want to study the designs in this book and the slope on which you want to place the terrace. Terracing design options will develop as you follow your intuition in reading the slope. Some people draw out what they want their terrace to look like, and drawing a plan is helpful in determining the materials you need to order. However, once you place the first stone, you will see how the elevations will influence your design. Every terrace I have built has its unique design; not only because I wanted everyone to have a unique terrace, but also because the character of the land and the slope was different in each case. Often the terrace comes together one stone at a time, delivering a design you could not have imagined. I start with a pick-ax and a flat shovel to carve and cut a flat "pathway" for the terrace wall. The terrace then takes shape--partly by planning, partly by designing and partly by faith.

This book is intended as a guide for your terracing efforts. Your God-given creativity and imagination applied to the slope and the materials will create a terrace of beauty.

I have coined terms for the types of terraces I have built. Examples of those terrace structures are pictured here:

## Isolated Island Terrace

This terrace is built on flat land or a gentle slope. The various levels are achieved by adding good top soil.

## Extended Island Terrace

An exposed foundation is the starting point for this terrace. The terrace extends away from the home.

## STAIRWAY ENTRANCE TERRACE

This terrace is usually built off an existing stairway. The terrace levels are built even with the top of the steps, every step, every second, or every third step.

## WINDOW WELL TERRACE

This terracing technique opens a basement window so light can come in, provides a place for plantings to enhance the view, and meets the fire escape codes.

## PLATEAU TERRACE

This terrace provides a transition or demarcation between two different levels of relatively flat land.

## FOUNDATION SIDE TERRACE

The objective of this terrace is to cover and enhance a large exposed foundation where the terrain slopes beside the building.

## PATIO TERRACE

Starting from an existing patio, the design of this terrace is influenced by what you want surrounding you while you dine or entertain your guests.

Terraces are usually built on sloping hillsides, but they also can be constructed on flat ground. The flat ground terrace is accomplished by dumping top soil in the spot where you want the terrace. You then create a terrace on the artificial "hill" you have created. Sometimes an extended island terrace can be constructed on flat ground, when the exposed foundation of the home or building is showing. Terraces also can be created on flat ground surrounding a patio or deck. A terrace can be constructed on flat ground at the side of a home or building if the foundation is high and exposed. Large terraces on severely sloping terrain and small terraces on flat or less severe terrain provide different areas for plantings and flowers.

## CONNECTED STADIUM TERRACE

This terrace appears connected to the home as it starts at a foundation or an exposed wall. A stairway is built into the design.

## ISOLATED STADIUM TERRACE

Isolated from buildings and built on a large hill, the various levels make this terrace look like stadium seating. These terraces have a minimum of three levels.

Dramatic landscaping terracing can be created on severe sloping hillsides where the change of grade is steep. Foundation Side Terraces, Plateau Terraces, and Stadium Terraces are achieved on these steep slope situations. Stairways, which are dramatic in themselves, can be worked into these designs. Stairways enable you to walk into the terrace for gardening and watering or to walk up the hill to a side entrance of your home.

## COMBINATION TERRACE

This terrace combines features of several terrace designs identified on these pages. It enables you to use two or more designs on different sides of the house, connecting them together.

## LANDMARK TERRACE

The terrace is built around a landmark, such as special tree, a school bell, a free standing church cross, or a windmill.

## DECK TERRACE

The empty space beneath a deck is unsightly for many homes. This terracing design adds beauty and character in front of that void space.

# WALL STRUCTURES

In designing terraces I use a variety of wall structures woven together to create an inspirational terrace. I have coined terms to identify these wall structures: Wall Step-up, Wall Step-down, Wall Split, Wall Split Turn-in, Wall Split Weave, Wall Split Weave-wall-feed, Wall Loop, Wall Stairway Mouth, Wall Stairway Fan, and Wall Stairway Shoot. In any given terrace I may incorporate more than one of these wall structures. Each of the structures (terms) is illustrated by the photos on the following pages.

## WALL STEP-DOWN
The cap level stones "step down" as the ground level changes.

## WALL STEP-UP
The base (bottom) level stones "step-up" as the ground level changes.

## WALL SPLIT
A taller wall is split into two or more walls creating shallower terraces, adding character and beauty to the terrace.

## WALL SPLIT WEAVE

A wall is split off to create another terrace and then weaves back into the main wall.

## WALL SPLIT TURN-IN

A secondary wall splits off and turns in to meet with the wall of the upper terrace, creating multiple divisions.

## WALL LOOP

The loop is a circular terrace added between two walls or below a single wall. The loops create ideal planting areas for individual shrubs.

## WALL SPLIT WEAVE-WALL-FEED

The top of one terrace wall feeds into and creates the bottom of another wall.

## WALL STAIRWAY FAN

Multiple wall splits fan out of a single wall to form the steps in a stairway.

## WALL STAIRWAY SHOOT

The step is an extension of the bottom row of stones, usually coming from a loop beginning at the house.

## WALL STAIRWAY MOUTH

A series of walls create a stairway mouth. The steps do not come out of a wall but are built between two walls.

# STRUCTURAL LANDSCAPING

Structural Landscaping is simply creating more than one terrace level, either on a slope or flat terrain, using materials to achieve the different heights and depths. This type of terrace design is seen in nature, on a much larger scale of course. It is seen in the colorful rocky layers of the Grand Canyon in Arizona, in the different rock formations in the Badlands of the Dakotas. Our great United States national parks in Utah, Colorado, and many other places display multi-leveled rock formations that are incredible, displaying God's awesome terraced creation. When you start creating the terraces illustrated in this book you will have a new appreciation of God's amazing creation.

Terracing provides a practical as well as beautiful solution for home and business gardens. From the many small pocket type terraces to larger planting areas in formal terraces, terracing prevents water run-off and erosion, holding the water in the various levels to benefit the plants. Terracing is practical also in that it can keep basements from flooding. Terracing creates a visually interesting garden place out of an uninteresting slope or a flat lawn. Terracing can give a home or property a colorful, interesting appearance even in dormant winter.

BEFORE

AFTER

# TERRACE DESIGN CONSIDERATIONS

There are a number of considerations in developing your terrace landscape design: lines, shapes, rhythm, balance, color, texture, and focal point. All should be considered in your landscaping design. A great terracing structure design doesn't just happen. You have to make decisions regarding the right material for your terracing project, the right color and texture. The use of lines, shapes, rhythm, balance, and a focal point with proper installation should deliver a great looking landscape.

LINES: Lines define edges in landscaping. Lines are created with plastic edging, steel edging, edge stones, a retaining wall, steps, a fence, the edge of a driveway, or a hedge of shrubs or trees.

SHAPES: Shapes create a visual interest in landscape structure. Shapes can be circular designs, quarter to half loops, half to full loops (and anything in between) curving in and then out, concave and convex. You can create just about any shape you can imagine.

RHYTHM: Rhythm has to do with the flow of design shapes and terracing style. Both should have some consistency throughout the terracing project.

BALANCE: Balance is extremely important in creating a good look in a terrace. You can have formal or informal balance. In a formal balance your terrace structure will have nearly identical shapes both to the left and the right. In an informal balanced garden the size and shape of the plantings can be used to balance the size and shape of the terraces. Another balance option is counter-balance where the left and right terraces may be at different levels.

COLOR: The colors used in landscaping are very important. Color is introduced with your choice of terracing material, crushed rock, and plant material. The colors that you want to bring out or emphasize in your home are the colors that should be chosen for the project. Different materials can be chosen to pull all the colors of the home out into the yard. It's even good to pull the color of a big visible roof down into the yard with a terracing material that matches it. When a home is all one color, a bold terracing material may be desireable. Some people prefer earth-toned materials. Good planning is important.

TEXTURE: Different landscaping materials have different textures. Some are rough and rugged, and some are smooth. Plant materials can provide a variety of textures as well.

FOCAL POINT: The focal point of your landscaping project can be created by a large wall, a stairway, a woven pattern, a large tree, a large shrub, or anything that draws your eye.

SCALE: The scale of your structural terrace should be in proportion to the size of the area of land and the size of the home or building to be accented by your terracing project. If the home or building is small, your terracing should be shallow in height and depth. The same is true if the land area is small. If you have a large home or building that has a lot of land area around it, your terracing should be taller and deeper. A happy medium can be found if there is a blend in your home and land.

MAINTENANCE: A spectacular terrace can be built using a great structural design, but if it isn't cared for after it is planted, it will never be enjoyed to its fullest. The terracing is done to enable the plants to grow well on slopes. It is a big thrill for me to come back to a terrace I poured myself into and see it in full bloom and well maintained.

VALUE: When a landscape terrace is done well, the end result is a property value that will increase as the plantings in landscape mature. A spectacular home with poor landscaping may not increase in value as much as an ordinary home with a spectacular landscape.

BLESSING: God created you to live in a beautiful garden, surrounded by many wonders of his creation. Planting, taking care of plants, and watching them grow, mature and bloom is a rewarding experience. Also, observing the different colors, shapes, and fragrances of the plants will never leave you bored because the garden areas around your home will always be changing.

# TOOLS

The tools needed for building an inspirational terrace are a shovel, pick-ax, rake, and a tamper for preparing the base on which to lay the stones. A sledge hammer and a blacksmith hammer or a large cold chisel are necessary for splitting and shaping the stones. A carpenter level is important to assure level walls. A caulk gun is used for the adhesive. Because the stones are rough, a pair of heavy leather work gloves saves your hands from scratches and abrasions. If your proposed project requires moving a significant amount of soil or gravel, a bobcat with a front-end scoop will save a lot of shoveling.

# CHOOSING THE STONE

I usually use one of four pre-cast, solid stones for my terracing work. They are all of a size appropriate to use around homes. The Windsor stone is a red color, the Pyzique stone is blue, the Arbor stone is brown, while the Regal Stone is gray.

WINDSOR STONE: A nice looking stone with a gentle tri-face. The 24 lb weight makes it manageable for building walls and terraces. A lip on the bottom of each stone helps achieve the proper step-back for each layer of the wall. This stone comes in a variety of colors and can be split and shaped easily because of its smooth top. When using the stone to build steps, a "vee" opening will appear between stones unless the stairs are built in a curve. The lip on the bottom of the stone must be knocked off when starting a wall along a foundation or turning the wall sharply. The Windsor stone, pictured at left, has a cap stone available.

REGAL STONE: A light weight (22 lbs) stone which is easy to handle. It has a look of natural, quarried stone, and its earth-tones blend into any landscape. The sculptured rockface texture provides a unique look that varies with the changing light of day. Pictured second from the left, the Regal Stone splits easily to accommodate your terrace design. Scoring at the line on the face of the stone makes it easy to achieve one-fourth and three-fourths stone pieces.

ARBOR STONE: The severe tri-face of this stone provides an additional dimension to the terrace walls. That dimension also creates a color illusion which can help in matching the terrace to the house. The lip on the bottom of the stone is useful in placing the stone, but must be knocked off in certain situations. The smooth top facilitates clean breaks when splitting the stones. The Arbor stone pictured second from the right weighs 24 lbs. Unless steps are built in a circular form, there will be a "vee" between the stones of each step. A cap stone can be used as well.

PYZIQUE STONE: Pyzique Stone is very versatile. It has the same face on both sides of the stone which enables you to flip-flop the stone to create solid steps without creating an open "vee" on the surface of the step (There is no "lip" on the stone). The three grooves on top of the stone facilitate bonding the blocks together with concrete adhesive. The weight of each stone, approximately 24 lbs, is manageable for the person doing the terracing. The face of the stone is a straight face, pictured on the far right. A chisel works best to split this stone.

In order to complete the terrace walls, you will most often need stones which are three-fourths, one-half, and one-quarter of the original size of the stone. The smaller stones are created by splitting the full stones. Score both sides of the stone with a blacksmith hammer where you want it to split. Strike it at the score with the sharp edge of the hammer until it splits. You may have to use the hammer to smooth out any rough edges.

It is important that your base layer of stones be level and that the stones lay flat. Remove the soil with a shovel as necessary to create a level base. It is best to level across three stones. The stones should slope slightly forward. Sand or small gravel is handy in leveling the stones in the base layer. If you want a straight section of terrace, use a string line.

# Adhesive

These photos show how to use a concrete adhesive for bonding prefabricated stones in a terrace. A caulk gun is very easy to use, but you need to be careful on hot days as the glue will come out fast. The glue is placed at the top rear of each stone. A drop about the size of a silver dollar works well (do not skimp on the glue). Be sure your stones have smooth, clean surfaces to assure a good adhesive bond. Where the sides of the stones butt together, adhesive may be applied to the sides of the stones as well. When every stone is bonded together the wall has tremendous strength, but still has flexibility to move a little bit in the freezing and thawing cycles. I have used the adhesive bond in northern climates where winter temperatures reach 20 degrees below zero and can approach 100 degrees in the summer. It has held up well even in these temperature extremes. In using the adhesive make sure the stones are dry and free from dirt.

Take plenty of time setting the bottom (first) row of stones. Using a carpenter level, make sure the front edges of the row of stones, and the back edges of the row of stone are level. The stones should slope slightly to the front so water will run off the stones. Once the glue is set, it is very difficult to pry the stones apart. Terry Mock, Ernie's Concrete Construction in Minot, North Dakota, says,"I was skeptical of this method of building a terrace, but after seeing a few terraces survive unusual conditions, I became a believer." It sounds elementary, but it is a wise building technique. Make sure you read the adhesive labeling before starting your terracing project. The bond, when it is done properly, is stronger than the cement itself. The adhesive will hold your wall together during the construction and after the project is finished.

# QUESTIONS AND ANSWERS

*Where do you get your inspiration?* For me, this is a very important question. Every terrace I have built was begun with a prayer asking for guidance in creating something unique for the people for whom I was working. I ask God for the vision for that particular project. Taking that first step in faith unlocks for me the gates of creativity. At times, while staring at a bare hillside I have seen a picture in my head as clear as a photo of a finished terraced structure design. I simply built what I saw. At times I didn't see the whole picture, but I knew where to start with the first stone. The hillside delivered the design as I followed my intuition while "reading" the ground and following the choices it gave me. The people for whom I build a terrace are an important consideration. Are they gardeners? Do they want lots of planting divisions or not? These considerations and the budget, together with my long experience in building terraces become factors in the final design.

*Do you use footings under your walls?* Footings are not needed for walls that are under 4 feet tall. This is the beauty of this terracing technique. You can split a 4 foot wall in two, creating two planting areas.

*Do you use gravel trenches under the walls?* Not all the time. I only use an inch of gravel base in situations where the walls are to approach 4 foot in height or in very poor soil conditions. Also, trenching on steep hillsides is extremely difficult because of the rapid change of grade. Using wall splits, loops, weaves, and turns reduces the height of terrace walls to 30 inches and under. In those situations it is appropriate to build the terrace walls on the surface of existing soil.

*Do you use pipes to drain water out of your walls?* I use pipes only when necessary to release water from behind walls that are filled from downspout drains or roof run off. In most terracing situations drain pipes are unnecessary because the walls are shallow. Also, I have used Pyzique Stone for most of my large wall terracing projects. It has a weep hole that releases water through the wall.

*What do you use for backfill behind the walls?* In shallow terraces I use a good, non-alkaline, black top soil. Behind larger walls that are going to catch a lot of water, I use a base of small pea-gravel or sand. The best backfill is a blend of these two materials. Because, the purpose in building a terrace is to provide areas for plants to grow and thrive, good top soil is an inportant component.

*Is it true that you use glue in constructing your walls?* There are some superb concrete adhesives called SF 400, MD 400, and PL 400. Out of the nearly 150,000 man-made stones I have installed, only a few hundred have been placed without this adhesive locking every stone together. This adhesive can withstand the freezing and thawing cycles. It also withstands severe hot weather. It has flex, much like a thick, tight rubberband. Sprinkler systems can be tunneled under the walls without affecting them. Soil can be lost from behind or below the walls in heavy downpours without affecting the walls.

*Do you ever get tired of building terraces?* Terracing is in my heart and is very rewarding. It's a great feeling to know that what you've designed and built will add beauty to peoples' lives. I get physically tired after a long season. But, soon I'm ready to size up another hill and start creatng another landscape.

## MY UNIQUE TERRACING TECHNIQUE

There are many different pre-fabricated retaining wall and terracing blocks or stones on the market. Each has its own prescribed method of installation with recommendations for heights, gravel trenches, geogrid, drainage pipes, and backfills. After choosing the stone for your terracing project, read the information about the stone. Depending on the soil condition and the annual precipitation, you may want to follow the manufacturer's installation recommendations. I have read the brochures of the major stone manufacturers and none recommends the method and techniques that I have used with great success. And, certainly none recommends building a terrace right on top of a lawn with no gravel trenches. However, I have built many terraces with my method and the pictures in this book show my work for many satisfied customers.

Using adhesive on every stone is extremely effective. Every terrace pictured in this book was built on top of the ground using a cement adhesive. Of the hundreds of walls I've built, I have had problems with a few walls because the foundations of the home settled, sometimes years after the terrace was built. Septic tank excavations can also settle over time. Settling of the ground is the worst enemy of a shallow terrace wall. Water pressure building up behind a wall is the second enemy of a terrace wall. If there is likely to be excessive water building up behind your wall, use a stone which has a weep hole.

The methods outlined in this book will not produce a stable terrace on very sandy soils or in areas of the country where there is extremely heavy rainfall. Consequently, I would neither recommend this construction procedure along a waterway or shoreline, nor for creating a pond.

The soil conditions and the water situation where you will be building your terrace should determine the materials and the methods for constructing your walls. If you are building your terrace on sandy or soggy soil or using wet and dirty stones, do not use my lawn surface placement and adhesive process. While this construction technique has worked for me, you will want to do your own research before adapting it for constructing your terrace.

# Isolated Island Terrace

The isolated island terrace is usually built on flat ground or a slight slope. The terrace is "isolated" in that it is not built against a home or a building. It is an "island," by itself. This terrace provides a point of interest in an otherwise uninteresting lawn. Drop a load of good top soil in the desired area and create the different terrace levels within the mound of dirt. Islands can be built in almost any shape you can imagine, creating terrace spaces for plants and shrubs.

This large, gently sloping lawn is ideal for an Isolated Island Terrace. The challenge is to create an interesting focal point on an uninteresting lawn. A truck load of good, black soil provides the fill for various levels of the terrace. *(See photo on previous page for finished terrace).*

An Isolated Island Terrace provides an interesting corner on a flat lot. This is a good example of the imagination of the owner/gardener and the terrace designer coming together to create an attractive garden.

These Isolated Island Terraces fulfill different purposes. One enhances the corner of a back yard while the other creates character at the front of a tract house.

Large Isolated Island Terraces can fill the space and create ample gardening spaces on large flat or gently sloping lawns.

# EXTENDED ISLAND TERRACE

The Extended Island Terrace is extended from an unattractive, exposed foundation. This terrace design is constructed on flat or sloping terrain. Not only does the terrace hide the exposed foundation, but also it creates a garden which enhances the appearance of the home or building. As the next pages will illustrate, the Extended Island Terrace is a beautiful design as seen from inside or outside the home.

This Extended Island Terrace is seen from the front step of the house and from the street. The terrace takes on a different character from various vantage points.

Two Extended Island Terraces built at the corner of a house create an interest center near the front door. The growth of the plants enhance the terrace as well as the house. In the lower photo the stone color is matched to the color of the Spanish tile roof.

The curves and loops of this Extended Island Terrace complement the straight lines of the house.
A stair creates a passage through the terrace. Below, wall splits create two flower beds on each side of the sidewalk.

These before and after photos show an
Extended Island Terrace built on a steep slope,
covering a stepped, exposed foundation.

BEFORE

AFTER

This Extended Island Terrace adds interest and
color to a plain exterior wall where there was a
modest, exposed foundation.

These are examples of an Extended Island Terrace built from an exposed foundation. The slope of the lawn, the size of the space, and the location at the house all contribute to the inspiration which created the terraces.

These Extended Island Terraces extend the level of the front step or walk, eliminating the sharp fall away of the lawn at the doorstep.

# STAIRWAY ENTRANCE TERRACE

The Stairway Entrance Terrace can be created at any home with a stairway going up to a door. Each step may be a starting point for a terrace level. The terrace can be built from every step, every other step, or every third step. The Stairway Entrance Terrace covers exposed foundations and provides planting spaces at the entrance to the home.

In a small, tight space this Stairway Entrance Terrace is constructed of six quarter loops, each starting at the level of one of the steps. In the Stairway Entrance Terrace some excavation is necessary to bring the top row of terrace stone to the exact level of the stair.

A view of the completed Stairway Entrance Terrace and the terrace with plantings.

The photos on these two pages show a construction sequence for a rather large Stairway Entrance Terrace.

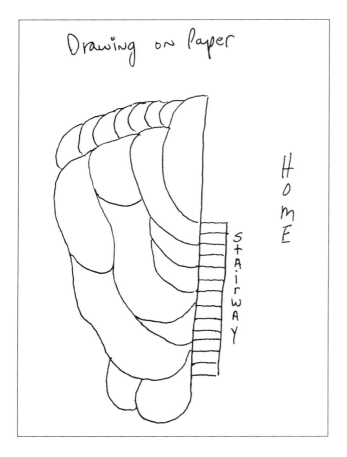

A pencil sketch of the basic shapes of the terraces is helpful in planning how the terrace will connect to the stairs and work on the hillside.

A long cement stair on a barren hill presents the challenge to creativity. Fifteen tons of top soil and 1000 stones are the raw materials for the terrace.

Note how the top level of the terraces are at the same level of some of the stairs. However, the way the terrace levels "connect" to the stairs varies greatly.

When the flowers and shrubs are in place, the once barren hillside takes on an entirely different character.

Two views of the finished Stairway Entrance Terrace.

## BEFORE

This set of "before" and "after" photos shows the dramatic change even a small terrace can make in the appearance of a house.

## AFTER

# Plateau Terrace

The Plateau Terrace is constructed on a slope between two flat land areas. This design technique is ideal for homes that are on sloping corner lots. The terrace can be isolated (self contained) or connected to the home or building. Spectacular designs are possible using this technique.

The top "before" and "after" photos show how the Plateau Terrace bridges
the upper level of the lawn with the descending levels of the sidewalk.

BEFORE

AFTER

The large Plateau Terrace in the photo at the right eliminates a small circular grade in the lawn. All mowing areas are now flat, and there are a variety of spaces for plantings and garden.

The Plateau Terrace on these lawns adds character to otherwise uninteresting sloping lawns.
Below, the terraces encircle large old trees.

The Plateau Terrace provides many interesting design possibilities.

# Window Well Terrace

The Window Well Terrace opens a below ground level window to light and air. The terrace also provides an emergency egress from basement rooms. Plants growing in the terraces enhance the view from the basement window; at the same time the terrace looks nice from the outside of the house. A vertical French drain at the bottom of the window well keeps the well dry.

The Window Well Terrace can be a simple window providing light and air to a basement room. Or, it can be a more elaborate means of providing visual space outside the lower level window or door.

One or two windows can be encompassed in the Window Well Terrace. The well created by the terrace can be rather small or larger with the terrace moving the soil bank away from the house.

# FOUNDATION SIDE TERRACE

The objective of the Foundation Side Terrace is to cover exposed foundation which steps up or down the side of a home. Whether severely or gently sloped, the foundation cut-outs provide the terrace levels. There are many wall options possible in these terraces that turn an eye sore into a fantastic terraced garden.

BEFORE

This "before" and "after" sequence shows the ugly foundation cut-outs which provided the form for a Foundation Side Terrace.

AFTER

When flowers and plantings are in place, the appearance is an improvement over the bare foundation.

The two Foundation Side Terraces shown here do not cover the entire exposed foundation, but contribute a visual enhancement to an unattractive steep slope as well as providing a stair to the upper level.

Both of these Foundation Side Terraces were built to cover concrete cut-outs at the side of the homes. While one is a more elaborate terrace, the construction of both terraces required the addition of top soil.

Each of these Foundation Side Terraces is built with stone of different colors.
Each exposed foundation presented different challenges.

# PATIO TERRACE

The patio is a place of outdoor entertainment. The Patio Terrace provides an environment for those activities. If the patio is next to sloping ground, a series of walls and a stairway may provide access to the patio so guests do not have to go through the house to reach the patio party area.

This Patio Terrace is built on a gentle slope below the patio. The home owners overlook the terrace from the patio.

## Before

## After

A multi level Patio Terrace is built on a steep hill beside the patio, providing planting areas and interest to the patio area.

These Terraces were built in locations to enhance the area around the patio, creating a beautiful outdoor environment.

# Deck Terrace

Decks are a challenge for the landscaper. It is difficult to make the area around and under a deck attractive. Some of the challenges are the lack of sunlight and the fact that the wooden posts supporting the deck cannot have soil piled around them. As the photographs in this section show, the Deck Terrace contributes to the beauty of the yard.

This sequence of photos show the construction of a Deck Terrace which nearly surrounds a small deck.

The Deck Terrace can be relatively simple or more elaborate, depending on the terrain around the deck.

An old rock wall (above) is replaced with a terrace (below)

Small terrace loops break the line of a long front porch deck and create planting areas at various levels.

These Deck Terraces are built out from entry decks or porches providing interest and color.

# COMBINATION TERRACE

The Combination Terrace combines a number of terracing techniques covering a large area. Some Combination Terraces completely wrap around the house. The Combination Terrace can start with an Extended Island which evolves into a Plateau Terrace with a stairway.

Stairs, plateaus, extensions, loops and quarter loops – all contribute to the Combination Terrace, parts of which may extend from or cover an exposed foundation. Mature plantings shown on page 58.

The Combination Terrace may include the Foundation Terrace, the Window Well Terrace, the Extended Island Terrace, the Patio Terrace, and the Plateau Terrace. The size of the area will determine the number of techniques to be combined.

# Connected Stadium Terrace

The Connected Stadium Terrace is usually built on a larger incline. The design may use a stairway to connect two Plateau Terraces. Often the terrace is connected to the house. Or, the terrace may connect a lower patio to an upper patio using a stairway.

This construction sequence shows a large Connected Stadium Terrace,
using two stairways to connect two levels of the lot.

This large, barren hill becomes the site of a Connected Stadium Terrace with many planting areas.
Blue paint was applied with a sponge to the face of the stones. See page 71 for completed terrace.

The stadium appearance can be broken with a mid–level patio
or by building on two sides of a home.

# ISOLATED STADIUM TERRACE

The Isolated Stadium Terrace is built on a very large hill. This technique always employs three terrace levels. The Isolated Stadium Terrace is a much larger version of the Plateau Terrace, usually having more than 6 steps connecting the levels.

The use of two colors of stone provides interest and identifies the various levels
for this Isolated Stadium Terrace built on a long hill.

This Isolated Stadium Terrace turned an unmanageable back yard
into a place of interest, both in summer and winter.

The Isolated Stadium Terrace built on a large lot creates the appearance of a large formal garden.
A few years of growth and the combination of stones and plantings create a beautiful garden (See page 65).

# LANDMARK TERRACE

The Landmark Terrace is used to set off a special item.
That item might be a school bell, a cross, a sign, or a
unique landmark. This terrace adds to a special tree or
provides an attractive setting in a public park.

These terraces create beauty and enhance the interest of specific "land marks."

Terracing creates beauty in barren places, inspiring all to find beauty in their lives.

# ACKNOWLEDGEMENTS

| | | |
|---|---|---|
| Cover | | Plantings by Maria Leier |
| Page 5 | Upper | 270 Windsor Stone<br>12 tubes of adhesive<br>8 tons of top soil<br>**Flowers by Morelli's** |
| Page 12 | Lower | 700 Regal Stone<br>35 tubes of adhesive<br>14 tons of top soil<br>**Plantings by Brendens's** |
| Page 20 | | 244 Arbor Stone<br>13 tubes of adhesive<br>15 tons of top soil<br>**Flowers by Bonita King** |
| Page 22 | Upper | 200 Pyzique Stone<br>10 tubes of adhesive<br>11 tons of top soil<br>**Plantings by Aberly's** |
| | Lower Left | 100 Pyzique Stone<br>5 tubes of adhesive<br>6 tons of top soil<br>**Flowers by Martinec's** |
| | Lower Right | 220 Windsor Stone<br>12 tubes of adhesive<br>6 tons of top soil<br>**Plantings by Gertie Haykel** |
| Page 23 | Upper | 1,100 Windsor Stone<br>55 tubes of adhesive<br>45 tons of top soil<br>**Plantings by Dakota Boy's Ranch<br>& Deslac's Valley Nursery** |
| | Lower | 600 Windsor Stone<br>29 tubes of adhesive<br>18 tons of top soil |
| Page 24 | | 230 Windsor Stone<br>12 tubes of adhesive<br>12 tons of top soil<br>**Flowers by Deb Middaugh** |
| Page 25 | | 300 Pyzique Stone<br>18 tubes of adhesive<br>18 tons of top soil<br>**Flowers by Bev Witteman** |
| Page 26 | Upper | 260 Windsor Stone<br>**Plantings by Hayhurst's** |
| | Lower | 220 Pyzique Stone |
| Page 27 | Upper | 225 Arbor Stone<br>13 tubes of adhesive<br>12 tons of top soil<br>**Flowers by Boyles** |
| | Lower | 120 Windsor Stone<br>11 tubes of adhesive<br>6 tons of top soil<br>**Plantings by Scott &<br>Jennifer Naum** |

| | | |
|---|---|---|
| Page 28 | Upper | 275 Windsor Stone<br>14 tubes of adhesive<br>13 tons of top soil & Pea gravel |
| | Lower | 400 Windsor Stone<br>19 tubes of adhesive<br>16 tons of top soil<br>**Flowers by Campbells** |
| Page 29 | Upper | 500 Pyzique Stone<br>25 tubes of adhesive<br>25 tons of top soil |
| | Lower left | 250 Pyzique Stone<br>12 tubes of adhesive<br>12 tons of top soil<br>**Plantings by Orlin &<br>Millie Backes** |
| | Lower right | 140 Windsor Stone<br>12 tubes of adhesive<br>3 tons of top soil<br>**Plantings by Church** |
| Page 30 | Upper | 195 Windsor Stone<br>9 tubes of adhesive<br>6 tons of top soil<br>**Plantings by Heilman's** |
| | Lower | 375 Pyzique Stone<br>9 tubes of adhesive<br>6 tons of top soil<br>**Flowers by Martinec's** |
| Page 31 | | **Plantings by Sheila Klein** |
| Page 33 | | 200 Pyzique Stone<br>10 tubes of adhesive<br>3 tons of top soil<br>**Plantings by Meyer's** |
| Page 36 | | **Plantings by Sheila Klein** |
| Page 37 | | 230 Windsor Stone<br>12 tubes of adhesive<br>10 tons of top soil<br>**Plantings by Ruby Walters** |
| Page 38 | | **Plantings by Maria Leier** |
| Page 39 | Upper | 375 Windsor Stone |
| | Lower | 1100 Pyzique Stone |
| Page 40 | Upper | 600 Pyzique Stone<br>**Plantings by Norblett** |
| | Lower | 650 Pyzique Stone |
| Page 41 | Upper | 500 Windsor Stone<br>**Plantings by Mehans** |
| | Lower left | 600 Pyzique Stone |
| | Lower right | 220 Pyzique Stone |
| Page 42 | | **Plantings by Clute's** |
| Page 43 | Left | 380 Arbor Stone |
| | Right upper | 110 Pyzique Stone |
| | Right lower | 750 Windsor Stone |

| | | |
|---|---|---|
| Page 44 | Upper | 575 Windsor Stone |
| | Lower left | 450 Windsor Stone |
| | Lower right | 142 Windsor Stone |
| Page 46 | | 800 Windsor Stone<br>**Flowers by Martinsons** |
| Page 47 | Left | 700 Pyzique Stone |
| | Right | 400 Pyzique Stone<br>**Plantings by Wheeler's** |
| Page 48 | Upper | 150 Pyzique Stone<br>7 tubes of adhesive<br>5 tons of top soil |
| | Lower | 600 Windsor Stone<br>35 tubes of adhesive<br>8 tons of top soil |
| Page 49 | Upper left | 250 Pyzique Stone<br>12 tubes of adhesive<br>5 tons of top soil |
| | | **Plantings by Mock's** |
| | Upper right | 900 Windsor Stone |
| | Lower | 1000 Arbor Stone<br>50 tubes of adhesive<br>18 tons of top soil |
| Page 51 | Upper | 400 Pyzique Stone<br>20 tubes of adhesive<br>10 tons of top soil<br>**Plantings by Aberly's** |
| | Lower | 190 Windsor Stone<br>9 tubes of adhesive<br>5 tons of top soil |
| Page 52 | Upper left | 180 Windsor Stone |
| | Upper right | 480 Pyzique Stone |
| | Lower | 950 Pyzique Stones<br>**Plantings by Mocks** |
| Page 54 | | 460 Arbor Stone<br>22 tubes of adhesive<br>18 tons of top soil |
| Page 55 | Left | 100 Windsor Stone<br>**Plantings by Deb Middaugh** |
| | Right | 650 Windsor Stone<br>6 tons of top soil |
| Page 56 | | 580 Windsor stone<br>**Plantings by Peterson's** |
| Page 57 | Upper Left | 320 Pyzique Stone |
| | Upper Right | 280 Pyzique Stone |
| | Bottom left | 210 Windsor Stone<br>**Flowers by Jennifer Dennis** |
| Page 59 | | 1,900 Pyzique Stone<br>90 tubes of adhesive |
| Page 60 | Upper Left | 350 Windsor Stone<br>**Plantings by Anderson's** |
| | Upper Right | 450 Regal Stone |

| | | |
|---|---|---|
| | Lower Left | 500 Pyzique Stone |
| | Lower Right | 820 Pyzique Stone<br>**Plantings by Davis's** |
| Page 61 | | 1,500 Windsor Stone<br>**Plantings by Cindy Haskell** |
| Page 62 | | 1,800 Windsor Stone<br>85 tubes of adhesive<br>55 tons of top soil<br>**Plantings by Greenheck's** |
| Page 63 | | 5,300 Regal Stone<br>280 tubes of adhesive<br>90 tons of top soil<br>10 tons of Pea rock |
| Page 64 | | 1,300 Pyzique Stone<br>65 tubes of adhesive<br>15 tons of top soil<br>2 tons of Pea rock |
| Page 65 | | **Plantings by Ann Wessells** |
| Page 66 | | 3,400 Pyzique Stone<br>170 tubes of adhesive<br>45 tons of top soil<br>8 tons of Pea rock |
| Page 67 | | 2,900 Pyzique Stone<br>155 tubes of adhesive |
| Page 68 | | 4,000 Pyzique Stone<br>200 large tubes of adhesive<br>100 tons of top soil<br>8 tons of Pea rock<br>**Plantings by Wilson<br>& Ann Wessells** |
| Page 69 | | Landmark Terraces |
| | Windmill | 670 Windsor stone<br>**Plantings by Kenmare<br>Garden Center** |
| Page 8 | Tree Ring | 65 Windsor Stone<br>**Plantings by Duane Tollefson** |
| Page 70 | Mohall Sign | 380 Windsor Stone<br>**Plantings by Anne Gokavi,<br>Pam Nehring &<br>Diane Witteman** |
| Page 70 | School Bell | 300 Windsor Stone |
| Page 70 | Cross at Church | 140 Windsor Stone |

## Photo Credits

| | |
|---|---|
| **Jerry Nordmark** | Page 29 Upper<br>Page 30 Lower<br>Page 33 Right<br>Page 51 Upper Right<br>Page 58<br>Page 60 Lower Right |
| **Steven Geffre** | Page 19, 71 |
| **Paul Nordmark** | all other photos |